AN ABBEVILLE ANTHOLOGY

FATHER
— AND —
DAUGHTER
TALES

For John and Rachel,
a father and daughter who made it!
— J. E.-S.
For my father — H.C.

First published in Great Britain in 1997 by Barefoot Books Ltd.
First published in the United States of America in 1998 by Abbeville Press,
488 Madison Avenue, New York, N.Y. 10022.

This book has been printed on 100% acid-free paper

First edition
2 4 6 8 10 9 7 5 3 1

ISBN 0-7892-0392-8

AN ABBEVILLE ANTHOLOGY

FATHER

AND
DAUGHTER
TALES

Retold by Josephine Evetts-Secker

Illustrated by Helen Cann

ABBEVILLE KIDS

A Division of Abbeville Publishing Group

New York London Paris

CONTENTS

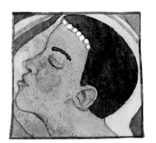

FOREWORD

Most folk and fairy tales have some aspect of the family drama at their center. In this anthology, the stories focus on the relationships that develop between fathers and daughters. How can a father love his daughter wisely and well? How can a daughter grow into an independent adult while still honoring her father? In every culture, these have always been dilemmas.

In these stories, the daughters of spirits, kings, viziers, rich merchants, hunters, woodcutters, and poor farmers all share common experiences. While the father usually sets the story in motion, he often disappears until the end. During his absence, the daughter can explore the world on her own and become self-reliant; in short, she grows up. Then father and daughter can reunite, forging a new relationship appropriate for the mature young woman.

Folk tales do not demand that their characters be perfect; the tendency to fail is accepted as part of the human condition. Instead, these stories work to repair and restore wholeness in a very imperfect world. This collection is full of fathers who fail through weakness or inflexibility, even though they love their daughters very much. But through error comes wisdom; the fathers' mistakes are the windows through which new and unexpected possibilities appear, often initiating a girl's most important adventures.

In most cultures, fathers traditionally embody authority, which in folk tales is particularly prone to fail. Fathers who rule over their daughters in these stories are assumed to be wise—yet they are often foolish, and need to learn from their daughters. Sometimes daughters must defiantly question their fathers' authority, relying instead on their own hearts.

Other girls in these tales have overprotective fathers who love them too much, keeping them from living fully. These girls must free themselves—often symbolized by their marriage, a sacred ritual in which the daughter leaves her father and unites with another. We might describe this tradition differently today, but it is important to understand its symbolic value in folk tales.

In the stories that follow, we see fathers struggling to love their daughters warmly and to receive love in return. Their responsibility is to encourage learning without betraying feeling; to protect without stifling; to guide without coercing; and to encourage independence. It is not surprising that this anthology is full of contradictions and enigmas. There is no simple equation, no single map: every father and daughter must create their own relationship. This flexibility is part of the excitement and fascination of these tales.

As the Dinka tale begins, "Listen to this ancient tale!" The authority of this voice has held us in its power for centuries, and we continue to benefit from the insight of the folk tales it relates.

Josephine Evetts-Secker
Calgary, Alberta, Canada
1997

THE FROG PRINCE

GERMAN

Long, long ago, when wishing still worked, there lived a king with a daughter who was brighter than the sun.

Around the king's castle grew a great forest. In the midst of the forest was a very deep well. When the days were warm, the princess would go out alone into the forest and daydream beside the well. Then she would play with her golden ball, throwing it into the air and catching it as it fell, gleaming in the sunlight. She loved this ball better than any other toy.

One summer day, the princess threw her golden ball too high. When it fell back down through the air, it missed her open hands—and dropped into the cold water of the well! Though the princess squinted hard into its depths, she could not see it at all. She began to weep helplessly. Her ball was lost forever.

In the midst of her sniffles, she heard a curious voice speaking to her. "Fair daughter of the king, why do you cry?" it asked. "Your weeping would break the heart of even the hardest stone."

She looked around in bewilderment, for she saw no one nearby. Then she noticed a glossy green frog sitting by the side of the well, gazing straight at her with its round, black eyes. "Oh, it's you, old pond-hopper," she said, wrinkling her nose. "If you must know, I am crying for my golden ball, which has fallen down into the dark well."

"I can help you," the frog informed her. "But what will you give me in return?"

"If you bring back my golden ball," the princess cried, "I will give you anything—my jewels, my gowns, even my crown!"

"I have no desire for your wealth or your golden crown. What I want is your heart," the frog said kindly. "I would be the happiest of creatures if you would be my friend and let me play with you. I want to sit beside you at the table and eat from your golden plate, and sleep with you in your soft bed to keep you company. Some day, I hope that you would come to love me. For this I will rescue your golden ball."

"What nonsense!" the princess thought to herself. "How can I possibly be friends with a frog?" But she said aloud, "You can certainly have what you wish. Only please fetch my golden ball at once."

"Do you promise to be my friend?" the frog asked, perching on the edge of the well.

Without a second thought, the princess snapped, "Most certainly I promise!" Impatiently, she stamped her foot.

Instantly the frog jumped into the dark water. After a few minutes, he came up with the golden ball and threw it on the grass. The princess grabbed it at once and ran merrily back to the castle.

"Wait! Wait for me!" the frog cried—but she was gone. Sadly, the green frog slid back into the water.

By the next morning, the princess had forgotten all about the loss of her golden ball. She played in the castle all day long, without a single thought for the green frog or the promise she had made. But at dinner time, as she sat with her father at the table to eat from her golden plate and drink from her golden cup, she heard the sound of tiny feet hopping slowly up the steep marble stairs. Then a voice she recognized croaked from the door, "Princess, daughter of the king, please open the door for me." The king looked up at her, startled. She ignored the cry, and with a pounding heart went on eating. But the king saw that she was afraid.

"Dear child, what is the matter?" he asked. "Anyone would think there was a giant outside waiting to pounce on you."

"It's not a giant, papa, but a horrible frog," she explained, shivering.

"A frog? What does a little frog want here?"

"I promised to be his friend!" she cried. "And now I am afraid. He rescued my golden ball when it fell down the well yesterday. I promised him whatever he wanted if he would fetch it for me. And now he wants to play with me," she wept, "and he is so ugly. Please send him away, papa!"

But the frog went on banging at the door and croaking:

Fairest princess with the golden ball,
Open the door when I come to call.

You promised me love,

You promised me play,

And here I come, to claim them today.

The king grew very serious. "My dear daughter," he said, "you must always keep your promises. Go and open the door and let the frog come in."

The princess opened the door and stomped back to her chair. The frog followed.

"Pick me up!" he called out. "I can't reach the table on my own." After a stern look from her father, the princess lifted him up to the table, where he sat beside her and ate from her golden plate. She could scarcely swallow her food, but he ate with great delight. When they had both finished, he said, "I am very tired now. Please take me with you to bed."

The princess could not bear to think of the frog lying on her white satin sheets, but the king said severely, "You must not break a promise to someone who helped you!" So she unhappily carried the frog up to her room. Rather than let him be close to her, however, she put him on the floor and lay down alone between her snowy sheets.

"Please let me rest beside you," the frog pleaded. Remembering how serious her father had been, the princess reluctantly picked him up and set him beside her. Then the frog sighed contentedly, and said, "I want only your heart and your friendship."

The king's daughter became so angry and afraid that she picked up the frog and hurled it against the wall. "You disgusting little creature!" she shouted. "Go away!"

Then, to her astonishment, the bruised frog turned into a young man.
From across the room, he looked at her with beautiful dark eyes.

"I am a king's son," he explained quietly, "and I claim you as my bride. You
should learn from your father to keep the promise you made to me." Then he
told her how an evil witch had turned him into a frog, until a princess would
set him on her bed with her own hands.

The princess looked at the handsome prince with surprise and wonder,
and sent for her father.

That very night a party was held to celebrate their betrothal—and the
princess danced most merrily of all.

ALUEL AND HER LOVING FATHER

SUDANESE DINKA

Listen to this ancient tale!

Beautiful Ayak was wooed by the herdsman Chol, and after they wed she gave birth to a daughter as beautiful as herself. But then Ayak died. In despair, Chol took the newborn baby on his lap and rocked her, while the people of his village said, "You can't do that. Find another woman to mother her."

Chol refused. "I will hold my own child and care for her," he insisted. He kept his daughter with him while he worked in the cattle pen, and he called her Aluel. He fed her on milk till she grew into a young girl. He alone took care of her and taught her to speak.

One day, Aluel said to him, "Father, why do you stay alone without another wife? Will I never have brothers and sisters?"

"Little Aluel," he replied, "I fear that a stepmother might not love you, or might make me forget you."

"It is not right to stay alone," Aluel said, and she continued to pester him with such talk for months. Eventually, he relented and married again.

"This is my daughter Aluel," he told his new wife. "For her sake, I did not want to marry. But my little girl has spoken wise words, and I have agreed to find another wife. You must take care of her, or you cannot live with me."

At first the stepmother treated Aluel kindly, but soon she secretly began to starve the girl. Chol asked, "Little Aluel, why is your belly like that? Aren't you eating?"

Aluel did not want to make her father unhappy, so she kept the truth to herself. Each time he asked, she answered, "Yes, of course I am eating, but I am not hungry now."

Then another daughter was born, and Aluel grew thinner and thinner. When the new daughter was old enough to speak, she asked her mother, "Why do you treat my stepsister so unkindly? She is hungry and you do not feed her."

Her mother was angry and shouted, "How can you say such a thing? I forbid you to say any more." So the girl did not tell her father or anyone else, and life became harder and harder for Aluel.

Then, one day, Aluel reproached her father: "Why have you never been to visit my mother's family? You do not even go to see how my grandmother is and to tell her I am well."

"It is because I fear to leave you that I never go far from this village," her father replied. "I am afraid that you will be harmed." Aluel laughed at his fear, so once again Chol did as his daughter suggested.

Aluel missed him sorely while he was away, so her stepmother decided to play a cruel trick. As the sun was setting, she told Aluel that she could see a man standing near the sun, and that it must be Chol. "Go, run to him and greet him," she encouraged the girl.

Off Aluel ran, nearer and nearer to the sun, looking for her father. She ran farther and farther, but the sun was running away too. When Aluel reached the big river, she fell in and started to drown.

But then she was rescued by the sun! "Where have you come from?" the sun asked, and Aluel told her story. The sun was very sad to hear that she had no mother to love her, so he took her home. He had two wives with no children of their own, and they would take good care of her. The wives were happy to have a child to look after, and grew to love Aluel very much.

Meanwhile, Chol returned home and found that his little Aluel had disappeared. He was immediately afraid for her and grew wilder and wilder in his despair. Soon, he was so wild he had to be chained in his cattle pen. There he sat, shouting all day and night.

Each morning and each evening, the sun passed Chol's cattle pen and saw the father's misery. Eventually, the sun told his wives that they must let Aluel go back to her father.

The next day, when the sun passed by Chol's village, he called out, "Man in the cattle pen! Listen to me! I am the sun, and I have seen your misery day after day. I have comfort for you. Little Aluel is not dead! She is living with two sun mothers who take good care of her. But I will bring her back to you."

Chol began to cry when he heard that his Aluel was safe, and he begged to know what had happened to her. The sun said, "I must hurry, so listen carefully. Cut some poles and make a high platform with them. In a few days, I will place Aluel on the platform for you."

Chol called the people of his village and asked to be released from his chains. When the villagers saw he was no longer raving, they were glad to set him free. Then he went into the forest to cut the trees to make the platform. After three days, the sun brought Aluel back to her father as he had promised. Chol secretly took her down from the platform and hid her in his cattle pen.

In another village that same day, a young man named Ring had a vision, in which he saw Aluel brought to her father by the sun. Ring had never met a girl who touched his heart. But when he saw Aluel in his vision, he said to his father, "I have seen the girl I want to marry. I must travel a long way to find her."

Then Ring asked his father to release cows to take as a dowry and he set off, accompanied by other young men from his village. When they arrived at Chol's village, Ring announced that he had come to marry Chol's daughter. The stepmother was delighted, and began dressing her own daughter to be the bride. Chol sat in front of his cattle pen, where Aluel was still hidden, and he entertained Ring and his friends. A bull was killed and roasted, but Ring would not eat.

"We will not begin to feast," he announced, "until the bride herself comes out to serve us water."

Chol was surprised at this and answered, "But my daughter has already served you. She is the bride."

"No, no. I desire your other daughter," Ring persisted, "the daughter who followed the sun. I have seen her in a vision," answered Ring. "I know where she is."

Chol smiled, and spread his arms wide. In a joyful voice, he called Aluel out of her hiding place, telling her to bring water for her new husband. Everyone was amazed to see her jump out from the cattle pen, strong and healthy! Aluel took water to Ring and his friends, and together they all began a wonderful marriage celebration—and way up in the sky, looking happily down on Aluel, Chol, and Ring, beamed the sun and his two happy wives.

THE GREEN KNIGHT

DANISH

Once upon a time, a princess was born to a king and queen. But soon after her birth, the queen fell ill. Knowing that she would soon die, she called her husband to her and made him promise to give their daughter anything she ever begged from him. With that she died peacefully.

The king felt that his heart would break, but he took comfort in his child. She was sad and gentle and liked to wander alone through gardens and woods, speaking to the animals and picking flowers.

One morning, while she was wandering through the forest, she came across a poor widow and her daughter gathering firewood. The widow was a sly woman, and the daughter vain and selfish. Not seeing this, the kindhearted girl stopped to talk to them. When the widow and her daughter discovered the girl was a princess, they plotted to make her their friend.

Whenever they met the girl in the woods, they spoke kindly to her. After a few weeks the princess began to look forward to these meetings.

One day the widow told her that they had hardly any money. They had to leave to seek work in a distant town. The princess was so unhappy to lose her new friends that she begged them to come and live in the palace. The widow pretended to think hard and then cried, "Why, I am alone with a daughter, and your father is alone with a daughter. Perhaps we could live together and take care of each other!"

The princess clapped her hands with joy and ran home to her father. She begged him to marry the widow so that she would not lose her companions. "They are the only friends I have," the princess implored. "The widow treats me just like a mother." The king could not resist her pleas and agreed to marry, against his better judgment. After a fine wedding, they all lived in the palace together. At first, everything went well. But after a few months the stepmother began to mistreat the princess and to favor her own daughter.

The king was distressed when he saw what was happening. "Alas, my child," he grieved, "I cannot bear to see you so ill-used. I should not have done as you asked. But now it is too late." He decided to send his daughter away so that she would be spared the stepmother's cruelty. "Take two ladies-in-waiting with you to my summer palace on the island in the lake. There you will be safe and I will visit you often," he promised.

The princess was sad at the prospect of leaving her beloved father, but there was no other way to escape the wicked woman and her envious daughter.

So she went to live on the island. It was a lonely life, though she was happy enough walking in the gardens and listening to the birds sing. Soon she grew into a beautiful young woman. But her heart was often filled with longing—for what she could not tell, though sometimes in her dreams she saw a handsome green knight.

One day, her father was sadder than usual when he visited her. "My dear, I must go away on a journey and I may not see you for a long time." He sighed as he kissed her goodbye.

The princess sighed too, and as they parted she said, "Father, if on your travels you meet the Green Knight, tell him that I greet him. I see him in my dreams, and I long for him. He alone can help overcome my sadness."

"I will grant your desire," her father promised as he rowed away.

The king was gone for many months. Though he met many knights and many kings, he heard no mention of the Green Knight. Eventually, he began his homeward journey, crossing mountains and streams, and finally entering a dark forest. As he made his way through the woods, he suddenly found himself in a clearing full of wild boars. A young herdsman sat in their midst, playing a pipe that soothed the animals so they fed peacefully.

"Whose animals are these, and whose herdsman are you?" the king asked.

"These beasts belong to the Green Knight, who lives far east of here," replied the herdsman, and returned to his pipe.

The king was delighted to hear about the Green Knight. He hurried eastwards for three days, till he reached a pasture filled with elk and wild oxen, also grazing quietly to the sounds of a herdsman's pipe.

"Whose animals are these," the king asked, "and who is your master?"

"I serve the Green Knight. These beasts belong to him," the herdsman answered.

"I must go to your master," the king said, hoping to find the knight his daughter desired. "Please tell me where he lives."

When he heard that he must travel another day eastwards, the king eagerly set off again. He passed through green forests and fields and then found himself in front of a great castle, covered with green ivy. When he rode up to the castle, the Green Knight came out to meet him.

"I have traveled far to find you," the king said. "My daughter requests that I greet you in her name."

The knight responded without surprise to the message, saying, "It is not for me that your daughter waits. She is sad, and was thinking of death in the green earth when she gave you her message." Then he offered the king a green book, saying, "Tell your daughter that whenever she is unhappy she should open her east window and sit there to read this green book."

The king thanked the knight for his kindness. After spending the evening as his guest, the king set off for home—but first he went to the island to give his daughter the green book.

That evening, the princess sat at her window, open to the east, and looked into the strange book sent by the Green Knight. It was written in a language

unknown to her, but somehow she began to understand the curious poems.
She read the first verse aloud:

> *The wind is restless over the land,*
> *Blowing the earth and sea and sand.*
> *Will love be promised, true and deep,*
> *Before the world falls into sleep?*

As the princess read the first verse, the wind blew past her and out to the
lake. At the second verse, the wind shook the trees at the water's edge. At the
third verse, her maids fell into a sudden sleep. Then a bird flew in through
her window.

The bird at once assumed human form and spoke to her. "Do not be afraid," he said. "I am the Green Knight, and I have come to listen to your sorrow."

The princess was overjoyed. Soon she found herself talking to him freely about her joys as well as her sorrows, as if she had known him all her life.

"I will come to you whenever you want me," the knight told her after they had talked for many hours. "When you are ready to rest, just close the book and I will return to my castle as quietly as I came."

She closed the book and fell asleep, dreaming of the Green Knight. The happiness of this dream stayed with her day after day. Soon she became bright and healthy and began to laugh and play with her ladies-in-waiting.

The king was delighted to see his daughter happy again, but knew nothing about her conversations with the Green Knight.

On his third visit, the knight gave the princess a golden ring and they were secretly betrothed. They had to wait three months, however, before he could ask the king for his daughter's hand in marriage.

Meanwhile, the stepmother grew very suspicious at the news of the princess's blossoming happiness. She had hoped that the girl would pine away and die while she was alone on the island, so that her own child would receive the king's affection. The stepmother sent spies to the island, but they all reported the same thing: everyone fell asleep in the evening when the princess sat at her window. Puzzled, the stepmother herself went to find out what was making the girl so happy. She thought that someone must be coming in through the open window, so she put poisoned scissors on the ledge and kept watch. But in the evening she too fell asleep and did not see the bird fly in; nor did she hear the talk between the lovers.

"I am so happy that we must wait only one more week before you can ask my father for my hand in marriage," the princess exclaimed joyfully to the Green Knight.

"And then you will come with me to my green castle in the midst of my green forests and fields," he responded.

When the princess grew tired and closed the book, the knight resumed his bird shape to fly away. Flying low through the window, he grazed a leg on the scissors. He escaped with a cry that woke the princess. Instantly, a wave of unhappiness swept over her.

After the stepmother awoke, she found her scissors and rejoiced that they

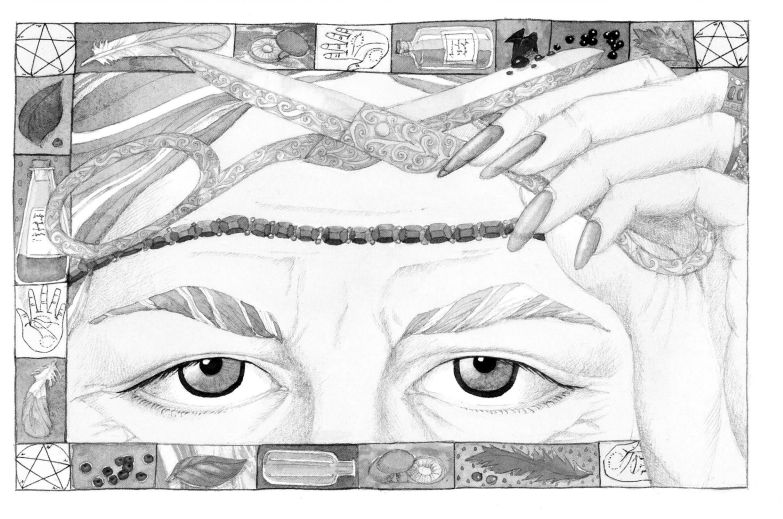

were covered with blood. Satisfied that her plan had worked, she went back to her palace.

The next evening, the princess was so weak with sorrow that she could scarcely open her book. When she did so, no bird came, though the wind rushed over the lake and through the trees. In despair, she tried to summon her knight the next evening, and the next. But no bird came.

One day, as she wandered in her garden, she overheard two ravens talking about the Green Knight. The first said, "How sad that the knight lies sick and only our princess can heal him. Yet she knows nothing of his wound from the queen's poisoned scissors."

The other raven asked, "But could she truly heal him if she knew of his fate?"

The first raven replied, "In the king's courtyard there is a nest of adders. If the princess can catch and cook these, and serve them to the knight three times, he will be cured. Otherwise, he will die."

As she listened to the conversation, the princess resolved to help the knight.

As soon as night came, she rowed across the lake by the light of the moon and stars. Quietly, she made her way to her father's courtyard, where she found nine adders and wrapped them in her apron. Then she set out on the long journey to find the Green Knight's castle. By the time she arrived her clothes were torn and dirty, and no one would have believed she was a princess. She entered the castle just as the doctors declared that the knight had no hope of recovery.

The princess begged to work in the kitchen, where she made a soup with three of the adders. When the knight drank it, his fever went down and he asked for more. The next day, she made soup from another three adders, and the knight was able to sit up in bed. His courtiers were amazed. On the third day, the princess made soup from the last three adders. When the knight drank it, he felt so much better that he ran down to the kitchen to thank the kitchen maid.

As soon as he entered the kitchen, he recognized his betrothed. Indeed, she had put on his golden ring, so there could be no doubt.

The couple embraced and wept and decided to marry at once. They sent a message to the king, explaining about their love and the stepmother's poisoned scissors. They asked for his blessing and invited him to share their joy.

The king was delighted that his daughter had finally found her Green
Knight. He left the evil widow and her daughter forever, taking all his
servants and many possessions. With joy in his heart, he set off immediately
to celebrate his daughter's wedding, and to live with her there at the Green
Knight's castle for the rest of his life.

BEAUTY AND THE BEAST

FRENCH

Once upon a time, there was a merchant with three sons and three daughters. The youngest daughter was dearly loved by her father, for she was kind and quick-minded. Because she was also very beautiful, she was called "Beauty." As they grew up together, her sisters grew envious of her and made fun of her at every opportunity. They resented the fact that Beauty was sought out by the richest and handsomest young men, though she always told them she was not yet ready to leave her father.

One terrible day, the merchant's fleet was lost at sea with all its cargo, and his family fell into great poverty. They left their fine home in the city to lead a simple life in the woods. Beauty quietly began to look after the house, caring for everyone as the servants had once done. Her father and brothers were grateful for this, but her sisters scorned her.

Many months later, the merchant's luck began to improve, and he returned to the city to attend to his affairs. The older sisters clamored for him to bring them back new dresses, but Beauty said nothing till he asked, "Dear Beauty, what can I bring back for you? You have worked so hard and so kindly for us all. I must bring you a gift, too." Beauty thought for a while and then said, "I would like you to bring back a single red rose."

Business in the city did not go well for the merchant, and he set off for home feeling discouraged. One night, caught in a terrible storm, he sought shelter in a castle that he could not remember seeing before. "I am sure I will be safe here," he thought, as he entered the courtyard. He called out, but no one replied. He decided to enter the castle and went from room to room till he reached a dining hall, where a fine meal was set out on the table and a fire burned brightly in the grate. Again he called out, but still there was no reply. Since the place felt so warm and welcoming, he sat down to eat, expecting someone to appear at any moment. Once he had finished his dinner, he felt so tired that he went to find a room where he could fall asleep. "It seems that someone was expecting me," he thought, as he lay down on a freshly made bed in a warm little room.

When the merchant woke, he found clean clothes where he had left his muddy ones the day before, and breakfast was laid out for him. The sun was shining, and before he left the castle he wandered in the garden to enjoy its beauty. Suddenly his eyes fell on a beautiful red rose, gleaming with dew in the morning sun. "I must take this home for my dearest Beauty," he decided, reaching out to pluck the rose. But just then he heard a bellowing roar, and a monstrous figure rose up before him.

"How dare you steal my rose!" screamed the beast. "How ungrateful you are! You must pay with your life."

The frightened merchant fell on his knees and pleaded, "I am truly sorry that I have offended you. I did not think it was theft to take such a small gift for my dearest daughter, who asked for a red rose when I parted from her."

"You should think more about what you are doing," the beast snarled. "You must be punished. If you go home and send one of your daughters to me in your place, then I will let you go free. Otherwise, say goodbye to your family and return to me within three months."

The merchant left the beast's castle and sadly made his way home, carrying the single red rose for Beauty. His children greeted him joyfully, but their happiness turned to grief when they heard his tale. Beauty did not hesitate for a moment, but insisted that she would take her father's place and go to the beast. But the merchant would hear nothing of it. "No, no, you cannot suffer on my account," he insisted to Beauty. "Just let me enjoy your company for a little while, then we will say goodbye and I will return to the castle."

But Beauty was determined to go in her father's place. "I cannot bear to live without you," she said, "If you will not let me go alone, I will follow you there. I have made up my mind." The merchant hung his head. He could not argue with his youngest, best-loved daughter.

Everyone wept as Beauty and her father got ready to leave, though the sons were more sincere than the sisters. They set off, and soon they came to the beast's castle. Food and fresh beds were ready as before, and to their amazement they slept well and woke refreshed. Beauty had dreamed of an old fairy woman who made her feel less afraid. Beauty explained the dream to her

father, and then said gently, "Now you must leave me to my fate. It must be so."

With a heavy heart, her father kissed her and departed. Beauty waved goodbye to him long after he had disappeared down the road. Then she began wandering sadly through the marvelous gardens and great chambers of the castle. She was surprised to see her own name on the door of one very lovely room, and she went in. There she sat on a little stool, buried her face in her hands, and wept for her father. But when she finally looked up, she realized that the mirror before her showed her the scene of his safe arrival home, and she felt less frightened.

At lunchtime, a meal was set out by invisible hands. As Beauty ate, music played and comforted her soul. In the evening, when she again sat down to eat, she heard the sound of a wild creature's roar getting louder and closer, and she trembled when the beast burst through the door. But her fear turned to amazement when he asked, very gently and without roaring, "Dear Beauty, can I stay with you while you eat? I will go away if you ask me to, but I would like your company for a while." Beauty was afraid, but nodded her head. The beast remained with her and talked very politely with her as she dined.

The next day was the same as the first, and so the days passed without Beauty being devoured as she had expected. She grew less frightened of the beast, finding him kinder and kinder as the weeks went by. After a while she was surprised to find that she began to look forward to mealtimes, when the beast would appear and sit with her.

Each evening after their delightful conversation, the beast looked seriously at Beauty and asked her to marry him. "Oh no," she always replied, "though I like you, I could not marry a beast like you." With that, he always smiled sadly and turned away.

One day, Beauty awoke feeling very homesick. She plucked up the courage to ask the beast if it would ever be possible to see her father again, at least to reassure him that she was safe and well cared for.

"Oh Beauty, your request troubles me greatly," the beast answered. "I have grown so fond of having you here and I am afraid that if you leave, you will forget me. And yet I cannot say no to you. You may go—but remember that I am waiting, and return here after one week. Take this ring so you do not forget me. When you are ready to come back, put it on your finger and you will be here at once."

Beauty's eyes were bright with tears. "Oh thank you! Dear, kind beast, I won't forget you. I promise to return before the week is over."

The merchant was filled with joy when his daughter suddenly appeared at his fireside. They spent such happy days together that Beauty completely forgot how long she had been away. Her sisters did not remind her, hoping that the monster would devour her if she failed to keep her promise.

On the tenth night, Beauty dreamed that she was back in the castle garden and saw the beast lying among the roses, full of grief and calling out to her. Beauty woke up, pale and frightened, and realized how much she missed him. "How unkind of me to betray my poor beast by staying away so long!" she scolded herself. She remembered the ring he had given her and put it on. Immediately, she was back in the dining hall of the castle, where the evening meal was ready for her. "How late he is," she said, as she ate without him. "Perhaps he is angry with me." When she was finished, she started to hunt for him, but he was nowhere to be found in the castle.

Then she remembered her dream, and hurried into the garden. There she saw him, lying alone and dying among the roses.

"Dear, dear beast," Beauty cried, throwing herself down beside him and taking his gnarled claws in her hands. "How I have missed you! Please forgive me and smile at me again!"

But the beast did not move. She stroked his rough face with her soft hand and he opened his eyes. "My beloved Beauty, I thought you had forgotten me. I am dying, for I can no longer live without you."

"Sweet, kind beast! Do not die. Stay with me. I will not leave you again! I will live with you here and be your wife." With that, she kissed him tenderly and closed her eyes.

The castle was suddenly filled with lights and music—the beast had disappeared! In his place was a young prince, who smiled at her joyfully. "Yes," he explained. "I am your beast. I was bewitched by an evil fairy and condemned to be a monster until a woman could love me. Now I am released from her spell and we can live together in peace."

Beauty's delight was even greater when they entered the castle and found her family there to greet them. Without a moment's delay, Beauty and her beast were married amidst music and dancing and love. The merchant embraced his daughter and the prince with great joy, and Beauty's brothers laughed and slapped the prince on the back heartily.

The envious sisters, however, were turned into stone statues, and they will stay that way until their hard hearts grow softer.

THE GIRL WHO HELPED THUNDER

NATIVE AMERICAN MUSKOGEE

Long, long ago, there lived a young girl named Brave Heart who wanted to be a hunter. She and her brothers had no father, but they had uncles who took good care of them and taught the boys how to hunt. Brave Heart used to follow her brothers whenever they went out to practice in the woods, even though they told her to go back home. She watched and imitated them and before long became a fine archer, skilled with the bow and arrow.

Every year, Brave Heart waited eagerly for the hunting season to start. More than anything else, she wanted to bring home some meat for her family. She dreamed of being asked by the men of the Muskogee people to go with them on their hunt, but everyone just laughed at her. Then, one fine autumn day, her uncles invited her to go with them into the hills!

You can imagine Brave Heart's disappointment when she realized that the men expected her to do the cooking while they hunted. Still, she held back her tears and tackled the job bravely. Before long, the men had disappeared and she was alone, tending the fire and stirring the meal.

Suddenly, she heard a strange, rumbling thunder. It came not from the sky but from the ground beneath her. She followed the sound to its source, a stream near the camp. As she approached, she saw a very old man wrestling with a water snake. The old man, Thunder himself, roared with each movement as he struggled. In the midst of the turmoil, Brave Heart noticed a bright white circle on the snake's neck. As she watched, the man and the snake both begged her for help.

The old man cried out, "Shoot him! Aim for the white spot! Save me!"

The snake shouted, "Kill the old man before his thunder destroys you. Save me and you will save yourself!"

Brave Heart was very troubled. "Whom should I help?" she wondered. "What shall I do? If I destroy the thunder, we may lose the rain that he brings with him, and then we will have no corn to eat. I have no choice but to kill the snake." Sadly, she put her arrow on the bowstring, and aimed as carefully as she could at the snake's white spot. The arrow flew into the creature's soft flesh. Instantly it released the old man and sank beneath the water.

Old Man Thunder pulled himself out of the stream and came towards Brave Heart. He was shocked to find that she was a young girl. "You are so young and so skillful," he said in amazement. "I would like for us to be friends

forever. Your people will soon need help, so listen to me carefully before I leave you."

Brave Heart paid close attention to his words. "Though you are a girl, you must go through the same rituals your brothers do when they need direction from the spirits. I will teach you a song that will give you great power to help your people, but you must sing it only when necessary."

Soon the men were ready to return to their village. Brave Heart followed her uncles on the trail, and as they walked she asked them to help her perform the medicine fast, eating nothing for four days to prepare her spirit for a special task. Her uncles laughed at her urgency. "You are too young! And, anyway, girls do not need to do such things."

But Brave Heart asked again and again, until the youngest of her uncles
finally said, "I do not understand why you have this thing in your heart, but I
will help you, daughter with a brave spirit."

In the weeks that followed, he set up the ceremony, helping her as an uncle
should. He stayed beside her all through the difficult nights in the sweat-lodge,
and led her to the place of fasting and prayer. During those four days, she
thought only of Old Man Thunder's words: "I will teach you a song that will
give you great power to help your people." Finally, the song came to her.

That winter, while the men were out in the hills hunting for meat, the
women in the Muskogee village learned that Cherokee warriors were
pressing towards them. When word of this reached Brave Heart's youngest

uncle, he ran towards the village ahead of the other men to look for his niece. He saw her from a distance, walking in a large circle around the village, and as she walked she sang a strange song. Four times she sang and four times she circled. Then she changed into a beautiful rainbow that formed a huge arc over the village, and also over the Cherokee attackers. The uncle watched, full of wonder.

"Look up at the sky!" shouted a Cherokee warrior, as he too saw the mighty rainbow arch above them. Suddenly, from the middle of the rainbow, Brave Heart raised her bow and started to shoot arrows of lightning around the Cherokee warriors. Thunder roared as each arrow shot towards the earth. All the Cherokees were easily captured, and they trembled as Brave Heart resumed her girl shape and cried out to them, "Remember what you have seen here today. Now go back to your own villages and tell it to your people. Leave us in peace!"

The Cherokee warriors ran away from Brave Heart as fast as they could, never to return. But the Muskogee people ran towards the girl, cheering and shouting her name—Brave Heart had saved her village!

The youngest uncle was proud that he had helped her. "We will tell stories about you," he said after Brave Heart told him her story. "You will be honored for all time as the girl who helped Thunder."

CAP O'RUSHES

ENGLISH

In times gone by, there lived a very rich man who had three beautiful
daughters. The eldest was as dark as midnight, the second had eyes as
green as a cat's, and the third was as fair as the morning. Their father was
devoted to them all, though his youngest daughter was his favorite.

One day, he returned from the city with three marvelous gowns as gifts
for his daughters. The first was covered with rubies, the second with
emeralds, and the third with smooth, white pearls.

The sisters ran off excitedly to dress themselves, and returned in splendor
to curtsy before their father. "Do you really like your gifts?" he asked over and
over, and they thanked him again and again. "We are always grateful for your
generous presents," they cried, and kissed him on both cheeks.

"Am I a kind father to you, my dears?" he asked, making them laugh. But

he asked again: "My lovely daughters, do you really think that I am a good father to you?"

"You are the kindest father in the whole world!" answered the eldest sister.

"You are all that a daughter could hope for," replied the middle sister.

But the youngest sister was silent, smiling with contentment at her father.

He gazed at his three daughters, and then asked his most important question. "How much do you love me? Can you tell me that?"

The dark sister caught sight of her rich gown in a mirror, and said, "Dear father, I love you as much as life itself." Her father beamed.

Then he turned to his green-eyed daughter, who was gazing into the emeralds on her gown. "Dearest father," she said, without looking up, "I love you more than the whole world." He glowed with pleasure. Then he drew the fairest of his daughters to him and repeated his question.

"Truly, my father," she replied, "I love you as much as meat loves salt."

Her father was disappointed and begged her to say more, but she stood silently before him. He grew angrier, and shouted, "So, you do not really love me and do not value my gifts. Get out of here!" With that he threw open the door, and she went out into the night without a word.

A maid ran out to give her an old cloak to cover her gown and a lantern to find her way. With these she set off into the night until she found herself at the gates of a palace much grander than her father's house. At a nearby stream, the tired girl pulled up rushes and grasses to make herself a rough dress and a cap. She put them on, wrapping her beautiful gown in the ragged cloak. Then she went to the kitchen door to ask for work. The

housekeeper pitied her and took her in, instructing her to scrub the floor. The other servants were amused by the new servant-girl's clothes, and began to call her "Cap O'Rushes."

A couple of weeks later, it was announced that the king was to hold a ball so the prince might find a bride. The servants were told that they could dress up and watch the dancing from the balcony. That night, Cap O'Rushes pretended to be too tired to watch the ball. But as soon as she was alone, she put on her satin gown sewn with pearls and gold thread, and went to the ball.

All who saw her were amazed at her beauty. "Will you please dance with me?" the prince asked, time after time. At the end of the ball, he was distressed to find that she had vanished.

"How splendid the ball was," the servants reported the next morning. "You should have been there, Cap O'Rushes, to see the most dazzling princess, dressed in a gown of satin and pearls. The prince wouldn't dance with anyone else." Little did they know that the mysterious stranger was Cap O'Rushes herself!

Determined to meet the princess again, the prince held another ball the next night. Again Cap O'Rushes pretended to be too tired, and went to the ball secretly while the servants watched from the gallery. This time the prince gave her a token of his love—an old, golden ring set with pearls.

The next morning, the servants again talked excitedly about the beautiful princess in the gown set with pearls. "No one knows who she is," they said, "and the prince would dance only with her. But she disappeared again, and no one knows where to find her."

The prince was so upset at losing his princess a second time that he held yet another ball. Once more the unknown princess appeared, and once more she disappeared. The servants reported that the prince was desperate with love for her.

In his sorrow, the prince became pale. Day after day he searched the countryside for his dancing partner, but she was nowhere to be found. The prince became sicker and sicker with longing for the princess.

"The prince will die soon if the princess is not found," the servants confided to Cap O'Rushes. "He isn't eating anything and is getting weaker and weaker. He wants to die, for he says he cannot live without her."

Cap O'Rushes went to the housekeeper and said, "I know a very special gruel that will strengthen the prince. Let me make some for him."

When the housekeeper agreed, the girl made her gruel and dropped the ring of pearls into it. The housekeeper took the bowl to the prince's chamber, and it smelled so good that he ate every spoonful. At the bottom of the dish he found the ring. His heart pounded as he asked the house-keeper who had made the dish. "I must see her at once!" the prince cried. "Send her to me now."

When the housekeeper sent for Cap O'Rushes, the girl quickly put on her gown beneath her cloak. Then she entered the prince's chamber. He took her hand and placed the ring on her finger and it fit perfectly. Cap O'Rushes threw off the old cloak and stood before the prince in all her splendor. They embraced and vowed never to be parted again. Their marriage was announced immediately.

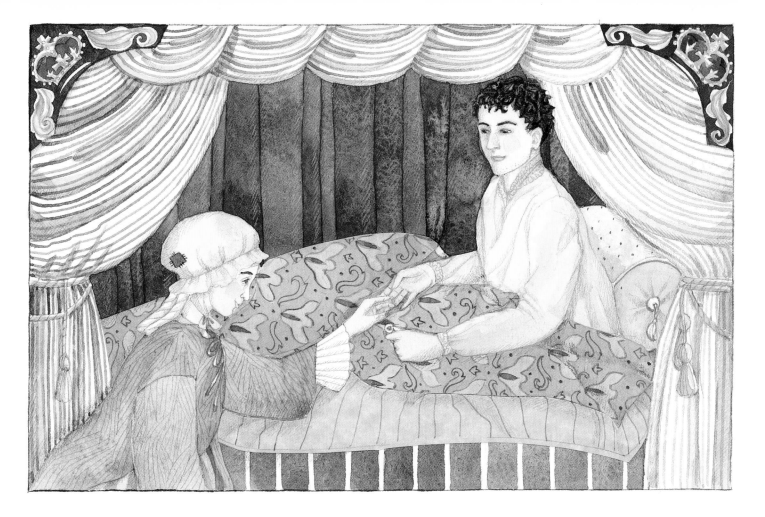

After much thought, the young bride asked her prince, "Please invite my father to the wedding, but do not tell him who I am." The prince did as she asked.

Cap O'Rushes' old father had long regretted his cruel treatment of his youngest daughter. While he had wandered through the country trying to find her, his other daughters had taken their fortunes and abandoned him. When he got the wedding invitation from the prince, he wearily came to the feast and sat at the lowest table.

The bride had instructed the cook to prepare two separate meals. The first was to be cooked without any salt, and the other was to be prepared

with salt as usual. At the feast, the saltless meal was served first. It looked magnificent, but the guests grimaced and refused to eat more than one mouthful; the food had no flavor.

The dull meal made the old man think about how sad his life had become without his youngest daughter. But then he looked at the radiant bride and cried out in amazement: Cap O'Rushes was his long-lost daughter. He ran to her, kissed her gently, and turned to speak to the guests.

"Dear friends," he began, "I have been a very foolish father." He told everyone how he had demanded to know how much his daughters loved him, and what his youngest daughter had said. "'I love you as much as meat loves salt,' she told me, and I did not understand. But now I know what she meant, and I realize that she loved me dearly." He began to weep.

"Dearest father," she responded, "I forgive you, and I love you still. Please rejoice with me and celebrate with us at our wedding feast."

"Gladly!" her father exclaimed, and the second meal was brought in. This food was more delicious than you can imagine, and everyone feasted on it joyfully until all the plates were clean.

SAVITRI AND SATYAVAN

INDIAN

Long ago, there lived in India a king and queen who yearned for a child. Finally a daughter was born, bringing them much joy. They named her Savitri, and watched her grow up with delight. Almost before they realized it, she became a lovely young woman. Savitri was also quick and clever, with a great talent for solving riddles and puzzles.

One day, her father said, "Savitri, it is time for you to find a partner. You must leave us and start a family of your own. Tell me which young man you desire for a husband."

Savitri replied, "I have looked around, Father, but so far I have not seen any man who makes me want to share my life with him."

The king was disappointed at these words and wondered whether her life had been too sheltered, living so happily with her parents in their palace. So

52

he responded, "I will gather pictures of every young man who might make a suitable husband for you. Your eye may find him, for the heart speaks through the face." He sent his court painters throughout the kingdom to make portraits of all of the noble men they could find. Savitri carefully studied all the pictures, but none of the faces pleased her.

The king did not give up. "Perhaps you need to go out into the world and see it for yourself," he said. "Then you will meet someone who touches your heart."

Savitri was pleased with this suggestion, and her excitement grew as camels, elephants, and horses were brought to accompany her on her search. For many months she traveled, searching through all the cities in the world, facing all the dangers and enjoying all the pleasures of her journey. But nowhere could she find a man to love.

She returned to her father's kingdom discouraged, but the king would not admit defeat. "You have sought your lover only in the cities. Now you must enter the dark forests and search there for a man you can love."

Again the king gathered together camels and elephants and horses to carry the princess on her journey, and he encouraged her with warm words: "Be courageous and open your heart to love!"

For many months Savitri journeyed from forest to forest, never finding the one who could touch her heart. She was discouraged and ready to return home when she entered the last, unknown forest. But there, in the middle of the trees, she came across a young woodcutter swinging his axe.

"My name is Princess Savitri," she greeted him. "Who are you?"

"I am Satyavan, your Royal Highness," he answered.

As they talked, Satyavan explained that his parents were old and blind. "Each day I chop wood for their fire; then I collect and cook their food," he said. "This is how I spend my life."

The princess was touched by his story, and for the first time she felt love in her heart. She returned to her father, joyfully telling him of her discovery.

After he had heard her story, the king said, "But the man is very poor, living in a simple cottage at the edge of the forest. Do you think you could share such a life with him and be happy?"

"I do not care for wealth, for rich foods, clothes or jewels," Savitri replied. "I want to spend my life with Satyavan, however poor he may be."

The king was pleased his daughter had found someone to love, and sent his

messengers to the blind, old couple to tell them that the princess would marry their son. When Satyavan came home from working in the forest all day, they told him the news. At first he was sad. "I have nothing to offer this princess," he exclaimed. "She is wealthy, I am poor. I love her, but she cannot possibly live in this poor cottage with me."

His parents comforted him by telling him their story, kept secret until now. "Dear son," his mother said, "you are also a prince. You are worthy of this princess."

"My brother plotted against me and took my kingdom from me by deceit," his father continued. "Then, having robbed me of my birthright, he blinded us both and left us to survive as best we could in the forest."

Satyavan was amazed, but rejoiced that he could marry a king's daughter. The king was so delighted that his daughter had found her bridegroom that he prepared a magnificent celebration.

Just before the wedding, an old wise man came to the king and warned him against the marriage. "It would be a terrible mistake," he said. "Satyavan is a brave and kind young man, but his destiny is to die very soon."

The king despaired when he heard this. He called Savitri to him and told her of the tragic prophecy.

"I fear nothing," she insisted, "and I wish to marry Satyavan. Together we shall face whatever life brings." However, she was a wise young woman and she asked the wise man whether there might be some remedy for Satyavan's fate. The Sage thought long and hard and then said, "You can spare his life for twelve months if you eat only fruits and berries from the forest—but then he will die. That is the only hope I can offer you."

The marriage was celebrated and Savitri began her simple life in the forest with Satyavan and his parents. Savitri's new family worried about how little she ate, but she only laughed and said, "Do not worry about me. I am very well and I eat those things I enjoy most."

Twelve months later, on the very last day of the year, Savitri got up in the morning and said to her husband, "Today I will come with you into the forest." He tried to argue, but she insisted. "I am not afraid of the wild animals of the woods," she said. "Remember, I traveled through all the forests in the world in search of you!"

They set off together, and soon they came to the very heart of the forest. Savitri's heart was pounding with fear, for she knew it was the year's end.

Satyavan climbed a large tree and was sawing its branches—but suddenly he lost his balance and fell. Pale with shock, Savitri helped him to the shade of an old banyan tree. There Satyavan lay, with his head in his wife's lap. And there he died.

Savitri sat in silent grief until she heard someone approaching. She looked up and saw Yamraj, the King of the Underworld, riding towards her on a water buffalo. He had come to take Satyavan's soul. When Yamraj finally turned to leave, Savitri cried out, "Dearest banyan tree, I leave my husband's body in your shade. Protect him for me. One day I will return to take him home."

Savitri began to follow Yamraj on foot. For hours and days she walked behind him, until finally he turned round to face her, saying, "Woman, why do you follow me? Go home."

Savitri replied, "You are taking away the soul of my beloved. I cannot live without him; take me with you."

Yamraj was annoyed and repeated, "Go home, woman. Go home."

Savitri ignored his words and trailed after him until he turned to her and said, "I will grant you one wish to be rid of you. But you must not ask for your husband's soul."

Calmly, Savitri replied, "Please restore the sight of my husband's parents."

Yamraj agreed to give back the old people's sight, but still Savitri did not go home. After many more miles, Yamraj cried out angrily, "I will not be followed! I will grant you another wish, then you must go away. But you cannot ask for Satyavan's soul."

"Please restore the kingdom to my husband's father. That is my wish."

"Very well," Yamraj said, "I will do that. But now you must go home."

So the kingdom was restored to Satyavan's parents, but still Savitri did not turn back. After many more miles Yamraj shouted in exasperation, "I have given you two wishes and still you pursue me! Now I will offer you a third and last wish. Remember, you must not ask for your husband's soul."

Her heart racing, Savitri asked, "Please let me be the mother of many children."

Yamraj replied quickly, desperate to be rid of her, "Yes, yes—you will be the mother of many children. Now stop following me!"

Even then Savitri did not go home. Yamraj could still hear her footsteps behind him. Furiously he shouted at her, "I have granted you all of your wishes, but you continue to pester me. You have the promise of many children. Why do you follow me still?"

"But how can I have children?" Savitri demanded. "You are carrying off my dead husband's soul. How can my wish be fulfilled? You have played false with me."

Yamraj was exhausted. "All right!" he exclaimed. "You can have your husband's soul back—just leave me alone."

Savitri immediately left him and raced back to the banyan tree where Satyavan's body lay in the cool shade. She felt the warmth of his forehead, and then his bright eyes opened—his soul had been returned! Savitri and Satyavan embraced. They walked back home joyfully, only Savitri knowing that the surprise of her first two wishes awaited them there.

THE BEAR IN
THE FOREST HUT

POLISH

There was once an old woodcutter who married a widow. Each of them had a daughter. The old man's daughter was just like him, hard-working and kind, but the widow's child was mean and lazy like her mother. The woodcutter loved his daughter dearly, but he was afraid of his new wife and never stood up to her.

The old woman treated her stepdaughter very cruelly and wanted to get rid of her. As winter came and the food supply dwindled, she ordered her husband to leave his daughter to fend for herself in the forest. With his heart full of sorrow, the frightened old man rode with the girl into the deep woods and abandoned her.

Soon, she finished eating the piece of dry bread her father had given her, and she became tired and cold. Then she came across a small hut. She knocked on the door to ask the owner for shelter, but there was no reply. She tried the door knob, and to her delight the door opened with ease. Inside, she saw a spinning wheel and a pile of flax set out by the window. Grateful at finding a warm place to rest, she sat down and began to spin. As she worked she heard a voice singing softly:

Wanderer, wanderer all forlorn,
Lost in darkness till the morn,
If your heart is full of light,
Rest here safely through the night.

Suddenly a bear entered the hut, and offered a friendly greeting. "Good evening to you, too," she replied nervously.

"Why are you here?" the bear asked. "Have you been brought by force or have you come freely?"

The girl began to cry as she told her story, and the bear stroked her face with his paw. Then he said, "Cry no more. You will be happy again, but you must do as I say. First, spin the flax into thread. Then you must weave the thread into cloth, and then make the cloth into a shirt. If it is ready tomorrow night, all will be well." With that, he left the girl alone in the hut.

By the light of the moon she finished the spinning, and then she slept for a while. As soon as the sun rose, she went to the stream to wash her face. When she returned to the hut, she found breakfast set out for her. After she ate, she sat at the loom and weaved till noon. Then she sprinkled the cloth with water from the stream and bleached it in the sun. Finally, she sewed the lovely cloth that she had made into a fine shirt. By evening, the shirt was ready.

When the bear came home he was delighted with the shirt, and asked her next for some porridge. While the girl prepared it, he went to fetch his bedding. In the kitchen a hungry little mouse appeared, begging for some food. The girl gave it some porridge and it scurried off.

The bear came back with his bedding and a pile of stones. After eating his porridge, he said, "Take this bunch of keys and keep jingling them all night." He fell asleep, so the poor girl started to jingle the keys, getting more and more tired. Suddenly the mouse appeared and said, "Give me the keys and I will jingle them, for you need to rest. Lie behind the stove where you will be safe."

Gratefully the girl lay down to rest, but she was soon awakened when the bear called out, "Are you alive?"

As she replied, "Yes, I am alive," he started to hurl the rocks around the room. The girl was glad she was hidden behind the stove, and that the little mouse went on jingling the keys. And so they spent the night.

At dawn, the mouse gave the keys back to the girl, and she jingled them till the bear woke. Seeing the girl, he exclaimed, "Bless you, daughter of the old woodcutter! Because of you, I will soon become a man again. I was once a rich king, but I was changed into a bear by a spell that could only be broken if some loving soul would spend two nights in this hut. Please be my bride, so I can take you with me to my kingdom. But first, please look into my right ear."

The happy girl peered into the bear's ear and saw a beautiful country, full of mountains and green valleys. She saw flocks of sheep and thriving towns and villages. "That is my kingdom," the bear said, "and you will be its queen. Now look into my left ear." There she saw a splendid castle, horses and carriages, rich clothes and jewels. "Which of the carriages do you like best?" the bear asked. The girl replied, "The silver coach with the four white horses."

The bear promised her, "It will be yours. And now you must wait for your father to find you." At these words, she found herself richly clothed and heard the sound of a coach arriving outside the hut. The bear disappeared just as the girl's father knocked on the door, for he had come to take her home. Together they drove up to their poor cottage in the silver coach, and the dog began to bark:

Bow! Wow! Wow! The rich girl's here,
Guarded by her father dear.
She glows with gold and gowns of silk,
In a coach with horses white as milk.

The old wife was amazed when she saw her stepdaughter so richly dressed. She pretended to be kind to the girl, asking how she had found such treasure. Of course, she was plotting the same fate for her own daughter.

The next morning the old woman sent her own daughter to the same hut. While she waited for the bear she, too, heard the words:

Wanderer, wanderer all forlorn,
Lost in darkness till the morn,
If your heart is full of light,
Rest here safely through the night.

The greedy girl grinned at the bear, and hardly listened as he told her that he needed a shirt by the next evening. The next day she did no work at all. When the bear asked her to make porridge, the same hungry mouse appeared, but she threw the spoon at it. Instead of jingling the keys, the lazy girl lay down to rest. When the bear called out, "Are you alive?" she woke abruptly and reached for the keys. Just then, a huge stone hit her and killed her in one blow.

At sunrise the bear woke up and stood in the doorway, stamping his feet till the hut trembled. As he stamped, he was transformed into a king, with a golden crown on his head. A golden carriage drew up outside, pulled by six sun-colored horses, and the king stepped inside.

He ordered his coachman to drive straight to the woodcutter's cottage, and there he embraced his bride. As they left the woodcutter's home, the old house fell apart and only a ruin remained. The king carried his new queen back to his castle where they lived happily for many years, without the stepmother to trouble them. The woodcutter went with them, and grew wiser over the years in his daughter's kingdom.

THE INVISIBLE GRANDFATHER

ITALIAN

There was once a fatherless girl who lived with her poor mother and two sisters. One day she said, "I can't stay in this hut any longer with nothing to eat. I am going to make a place for myself in the world." And she started walking, with nothing but the rags on her back.

Just when she felt she could walk no further, she came to a palace. To her surprise, the door was wide open. "I will go straight in," she thought, "for they might need a servant." No one came to receive her, so she called out, "Is there anyone at home to give work to a poor girl?" Her call echoed through the great halls, but no one replied. She found the kitchen, and looked in the cupboards until she found some bread and rice and a little wine. "This is enough for a feast," she said.

As soon as she spoke, two hands appeared to set the table. Then they made a delicious meal for her. "How lucky I am," the girl thought, as she sat down to eat. When she finished she said to herself, "I am tired after my journey. I would like to sleep."

She wandered through the palace looking for a place to rest, and found a room with a beautiful canopied bed. "How good it would be to sleep in that!" she exclaimed. Yawning, she lay down. The next thing she knew, it was already morning.

As soon as she awoke, the same two hands brought her breakfast. Then she started to explore the lonely palace again. Finding closets full of beautiful gowns, she threw her rags aside and put on a jeweled dress. Then she caught sight of herself in a mirror. "How beautiful I look!" she exclaimed. And indeed, she did.

Wearing her fine clothes, she walked out into the garden just as a king drove by in his carriage. When he saw her, his heart was touched and he longed to talk with her. He stopped his carriage and approached her. "Good morning, sweet lady," he began. "Please, tell me your name. And whose palace is this? Whose daughter are you?" Then he asked permission to visit her again.

The girl was impressed by his good manners and replied, "I have no parents, but if you return here another day, I will have answers to your questions." The king bowed low and left in his carriage.

The girl went straight to the huge fireplace in the center of the great hall, and began to talk to it. "Kind sir," she asked curiously, "I don't know where I am or how I found this place. I can see no one, but I have been well provided for and I am deeply grateful. Please tell me what I must do, for a king wishes to court me."

To her surprise, a deep voice spoke from the chimney. "Beautiful you are and even more beautiful you will become. Tell the king that your grandfather is sick and lonely, and is happy for you to marry—only you must not delay. Go to him with this message, most lovely girl whose loveliness will increase."

The next day when the king arrived, the girl had grown more beautiful than he remembered. She called to him from her balcony, saying, "My grandfather is willing for you to court me, as long as the marriage is not delayed." The king was delighted and they spent many hours talking together.

The next week, the girl went to the chimney again and asked, "Dear Grandfather, do you think we have courted long enough, and that we may now marry?"

The grandfather replied, "Beautiful you are and even more beautiful you will become! Yes, it is time to marry. But when you leave, you must be absolutely sure to take with you every single item that is in the palace. Leave nothing behind, most lovely girl whose loveliness will increase."

The girl swept out the palace and removed everything, but she forgot to take the necklace she planned to wear. When the carriage arrived for her, she went to the fireplace and said, "Dearest Grandfather, now I will leave you, for my bridegroom has come for me. I have done all you asked me to do. The palace is empty and I will depart."

"Thank you," the deep voice replied. "Now leave me alone."

So the girl left with the king, who was amazed that her beauty was greater than ever. But as they drove away, the girl suddenly remembered the necklace,

and insisted that they go back to retrieve it. She rushed back into the palace and called out to the fireplace, "Dear Grandfather, I am so sorry! I forgot one thing, the necklace I intended to wear. I have come back for it."

An angry voice cried out to her as she put the gold chain around her neck, "Be off with you, you ugly, bearded woman!" As soon as the words were spoken, she felt her face become hairy and found she had grown a beard that reached down to her waist. In terror she ran out to her bridegroom, who was also horrified by what he saw. "I can't take you back to my castle like this!" he said. "We must go to my house in the forest and decide what to do."

Each day the king came to the forest to visit his betrothed. Rumors soon spread that he was courting an ugly, bearded woman. But the king still loved her.

One day the girl said to him, "Please bring me a black velvet dress and a black veil to cover my face, for I must go to speak with my grandfather again." The clothes were brought to her, and the girl drove back to the palace. She approached the fireplace cautiously. "Grandfather," she whispered, "it's me."

"You hideous thing! What do you want from me?" he grunted.

"Dear Grandfather, hear me," she begged. "My life is ruined. You are responsible for my grief."

"Me, responsible?" he repeated. "You were the one to leave something behind when I told you to take everything away from the palace."

"O Grandfather, be merciful!" the girl cried. "I do not ask for the beauty that increased each day as I lived in your palace. I just want to be the girl I was when I first came here. Grandfather, please help me and make me the way I used to be."

The grandfather heard her pleas and relented. "Very well, so it will be. But are you certain you have not left anything behind this time?"

"I have the necklace in my hand," she cried, "and the palace is quite, quite empty."

Then a gentle, deep voice echoed from the chimney, "Beautiful you are and even more beautiful you will become. Go and marry your king, most lovely girl whose loveliness will increase."

She ran back to her beloved with her beauty renewed, her heart filled with love for her grandfather and her bridegroom both. The king was overjoyed and took her back to his castle, where the whole kingdom rejoiced as they were married. Hand in hand, they appeared before their people, who shouted, "Long live our new King and Queen!"

SCHEHERAZADE

ARABIAN

In the chronicles of times long past, it is written that once there reigned in Arabia a king called Shah Shehriyar. For years, the Shah and his wife lived happily. Then his wife betrayed him. Full of bitterness and anger, Shah Shehriyar swore that he would never remarry. To ensure that he was not fooled again, he demanded that a young woman visit him each night, and that her head be chopped off the next morning. He ordered his vizier to find these women, threatening to kill him if he failed to obey.

Day after day, the Shah did this dreadful deed. Soon the citizens grew to fear their ruler. Fathers and mothers cried out against his fury, but nothing could end his bitterness. Soon there were only two maidens left in the city—the daughters of the vizier himself.

The vizier trembled with fear over his next audience with Shah Shehriyar, for he could not send his daughters to their death—but if the Shah's rage was not satisfied, he knew he would lose his own head. In his anxiety, the vizier confided in his daughters, Scheherazade and Dunyazade. They were very alarmed to hear of their fate and feared for their lives.

Scheherazade was silent for a while. She was a brave and clever young woman who had read all the stories of her people and had become extremely wise.

"Father, I am most distressed about what has happened to the innocent young women in this kingdom," she said. "There must be a way to end this cruelty." After some thought, she continued. "I myself will go to our Shah! Take me to him, and I will deliver us all from his anger."

"In the name of Allah," cried out her father, "do not speak so foolishly. You would die just as all the others have died."

But all she would say was, "It must be so. It will be so."

The vizier used every argument he could think of to put this notion out of Scheherazade's head, but her heart was set on it. All she would say was, "It must be so. It will be so."

Then she added, "If you won't take me to the Shah, I will go alone and tell him that you refuse to bring me to fulfill his demands." The vizier no longer dared deny her request.

Then Scheherazade told her sister, Dunyazade, "Be sure to be alert tonight. When the Shah sends for you, come quickly. When I greet you, ask me to tell you a story to pass the night before I must lose my head."

With that she gave herself to the Shah, who was delighted by her beauty and wit. But after he had enjoyed her company, she began to weep. When he asked what troubled her, she said, "Since I must die tomorrow, I would like to see my sister, Dunyazade, for the last time."

The Shah sent for Dunyazade at once and she came as planned, greeting her sister with tears in her eyes. She said, "Dear sister, let us spend this sad night telling stories together. It will help pass the time till dawn."

With the Shah's permission, Scheherazade began her tale:

"In times past, there was a merchant who was rich beyond compare. As he traveled through a hot country, he came upon a most beautiful garden and he sat beneath a walnut tree to enjoy its shade. Suddenly. . . ."

And so the story began. The Shah listened eagerly as Scheherazade's beautiful voice rose and fell with sorrow or excitement. She went on spinning her tale until she saw the light begin to glow through the window. When she stopped, the Shah was very disappointed.

"What a marvelous tale!" he exclaimed. "Never have I heard the like."

"By Allah," Scheherazade replied, "this tale is nothing compared to the one I would tell tomorrow night—but I must die with the morning light, so that cannot be."

"I must hear another tale this coming night," the Shah decided, and he called in his vizier. "Be sure to let Scheherazade rest today, for I want to hear another story tonight."

The vizier and his daughters rejoiced at the one extra day of life Scheherazade had won. It was to be the first of many, for so began the thousand and one tales Scheherazade told to entertain the Shah.

Night after night the Shah was moved by Scheherazade's stories, and as the days turned into years, she bore him three children. Then, as the sun

rose one morning, she said, "O Shah, for many nights I have entertained you with tales of magic and love. I have told stories of war and wisdom, and now I have a request. May I ask just one favor?"

"Most surely, fair Scheherazade, ask me what you will. By Allah, I will grant your request."

"Please," she said, "bring my children to me first."

When the nurses brought the children to the Shah's rooms, Scheherazade said boldly, "O Shah, these are your children. I beg that you will spare my life so I can take care of them. I long to give them the love of a mother and raise strong sons and daughters."

Then Shah Shehriyar spoke solemnly to her. "Precious and clever Scheherazade, I pardoned you even before these children were born, for

you are generous and fair and deserve to live a long life. You have wooed me with wit and wisdom and with the magic of your stories. I beg you to marry me with feasting and rejoicing, that all may honor you."

And so it was announced, and the kingdom was filled with the music and laughter of the wedding feast. The vizier was overjoyed that his daughter was spared, and even more that her wisdom had tamed the Shah's angry heart and saved the city's innocent maidens.

So praise be to Allah, who will grant us, and all stories, a good end.

NOTES

Today, fatherhood seems more complicated and less clearly defined than it did in the past. But while changing expectations create insecurity, they also allow for richer possibilities. Because folk tales explore family relationships, they can help us better understand the father-daughter bond—what is timeless and unchangeable, and what can be negotiated as we evolve. The following notes highlight some of the important issues working through this collection, and through the lives of every father and daughter.

DAUGHTERS OF KINGS AND OF POOR MEN

Folk tales suggest that a daughter is marked by the personality, character, and social position of her father from the day she is born. Whether he is a king or a poor farmer, she goes out into the world under his banner. In practical terms, this determines her initial understanding of her place and status in the world. But girls also develop an inward, symbolic sense of who they are, growing into new phases as they develop. A girl might feel like a rich man's daughter at one moment, and the child of a poor man at another, as her moods shift and her inner sense of identity changes. A king's daughter, like Savitri, can feel confident of her royal value even in a poor woodcutter's cottage; so can the daughter of a poor man, if she has a sense of her father's riches in other aspects. A daughter who feels her father's poverty, however, must have her own value affirmed before she can succeed in the world.

These emotions are universal, and do not hinge on literal wealth or lack of it. For example, confident and generous men are "kings," while the powerless and weak-willed are impoverished. The Green Knight found his bride lonely and sad on her island despite her father's wealth and royalty; she was as confined as Aluel in her African cattle pen.

THE FATHER AS PROTECTOR AND PROVIDER

These stories often betray the simple faith that a father can shelter his daughter from the dangers of life. Fathers who feel powerless leave their daughters to fend for themselves, like the poor woodcutter in "The Bear in the Forest Hut" who leaves his daughter in the woods. But such girls often change their destiny when they are forced to rely on their inner resources, especially in the great forest.

Fairy tales even question how much a father should try to protect his daughter. Kind fathers whose love makes them overprotective can undermine their daughters' potential just as much as cruel fathers who actively hinder their daughters' efforts. A father's task is to encourage his daughter's sense of purpose and power, her ability to pursue her goals, ambitions, and desires—even when this requires him to ignore his daughter's wishes. In "The Frog Prince," the king shatters the princess's belief that he will protect her from her fear and from her promise. Wisely, he pushes her to confront the fear and honor the promise, developing her sense of power and trustworthiness.

Fathers traditionally provide "daily bread," emotionally as well as literally. When all is well, a daughter can take this loving support for granted. Fathers are occasionally excessive in their generosity, offering special gifts—but sometimes with very mixed motives. In "Cap O'Rushes," the youngest daughter understands the difference between a genuine gift and manipulation; she does not let her father buy her heart to satisfy his need for power.

"Cap O'Rushes" also explores the worst possible crisis for a daughter: being thrown out from her father's care, so that she must provide for herself. Many folk tales use this situation to show how such girls not only survive by their own wit, but actually discover lives far richer than their fathers could have provided.

The Father and Marriage

In many folk tales, widowed fathers are left to care for their motherless daughters. These girls sometimes come to embody the father's love for his lost wife, as in "Aluel and Her Loving Father" and "The Green Knight." This can lead to incestuous overtones, implied in "Beauty and the Beast," for example, by the gift of the red rose, the flower of love. But daughters cannot love their fathers as wives. Folk tales insist that good fathers take the risk of remarrying, despite fears about step-family relationships. When the father remarries, he frees his daughter emotionally.

Good fathers in folk tales encourage their daughters to leave them, to unite with their own partners. The daughter's marriage represents her separation from her father and a maturing independence. In "The Invisible Grandfather," the paternal voice supports the girl's marriage and insists that she become queen of her own kingdom, leaving him alone in his hearth. Savitri's father also knows that the right partner exists for his daughter, and sends her out to find Satyavan.

Daughters are sometimes reluctant to marry in fairy tales, often indicating an immature attachment to their fathers; Beauty says explicitly that she is not ready to leave her father or his home. Since the stories demand independence, the daughter must overcome this refusal, making an active choice to grow into the next phase of her development.

Feeling and Transformation

In several stories, a prince is bewitched into animal form and must interact with a woman before he can resume his human shape. It is not surprising that a daughter reluctant to leave her father would see her suitor in a monstrous form; before she can see the prince in his true form, her ties to her father must be weakened. Often, it is the father himself who instigates these changes, as in "Beauty and the Beast" and "The Frog Prince."

In each case, the spell is broken once the beast is allowed to relate to the growing woman. Often, it is strong feeling that causes the prince's transformation. The eruption of genuine feeling is always allowed, be it attraction or replusion: kissing the beast or hurling the frog against the wall.

Brave Heart's transformation is very different, though still linked to strong emotions; her passion, courage, and sense of authority give her special powers. She allies herself with the spirit of nature and the sky's energy when she delivers Thunder from the serpent, and she is transformed into a protective rainbow when her people are threatened.

The Father, Culture, and Authority

Traditional moral and cultural values are usually carried by father figures in fairy tales. His is a world of thought, principle, action, and political necessity. Attentive fathers use these values to nourish the minds, spirits, and characters of their daughters. The daughter, often compelled by emotion, has to find her own way through this world. In "The Frog Prince," for example, the princess must reconcile her own feelings with the principles her father teaches.

The codes of behavior that fathers enforce create a necessary sense of security. However, the tales often sabotage this very security. Scheherazade's father taught her to love the culture of her people, its poetry, history, and traditions—but this world becomes terrifying when the Shah acts tyrannically in following his own principles. Still, since she was raised to understand the world of men in her culture, Scheherazade can creatively adapt their system in ways the men themselves cannot see, particularly by playing with the power of words. In this way, Scheherazade saves her own life; Savitri used similar skills to save the life of her husband.

In some fairy tales, the father's authority is flawed; he is not wise. In these cases, the daughters must subvert his authority. They use their superior wisdom in distinctly feminine ways, despite their apparent vulnerability and dependence. Cap O' Rushes, for example, puts her intelligence to good use, revealing the folly of her father through a simple, domestic metaphor.

SURROGATE FATHERS

Folk tales do not deal only with biological fatherhood. In this collection we find kings, spirits, gods, uncles, and other male figures who symbolically represent different aspects of the father.

Kings, like the Shah, are fathers to their kingdoms. This bond can work like the father-daughter relationship, especially in the use and abuse of power. Once Scheherazade has tenderly outwitted the Shah, he can become a kind father to his own children and to his subjects.

In many cultures, uncles can assume some aspects of a father's role. This type of uncle acts as a good father to Brave Heart, giving her spiritual help after her encounter with Thunder. He assists the girl in her quest so she can find her unique destiny, by means of rituals usually reserved for boys of her tribe.

When a father is missing, his daughter might imagine a grandiose father figure to compensate for her loss. In the Italian story, the girl creates an invisible grandfather to help her develop a sense of her own value, as a good father would have.

Yamraj, King of the Underworld in "Savitri and Satyavan," carries off Savitri's husband, representing some of the dark forces of fatherhood—those that seek to keep daughters for themselves. But Savitri's wise father raised her to be able to leave his palace and unite with a partner, so she is strong enough to resist Yamraj and reclaim her husband.

IN CONCLUSION

In folk tales, a father is a necessary force in his daughter's life, even when he does nothing but set the story in motion. The daughter's successful growth into womanhood is significantly affected by his presence or absence. The daughters these tales celebrate can use the experiences they had with their fathers to help them engage positively with all forms of masculinity, both within themselves and in the outside world.